A Collection of Poems Spoken into The Night

Dedications

This book would not have been possible without the peer pressure from the ones I love and admire so dearly. The encouragement to be fearless and heard will never go unnoticed.

I am a mirror to their strengths and a safe place for their weaknesses.

To the souls who melted into mine; thank you.

To the souls who collided with mine; it was a pleasure.

And to the ones who barged past the boundaries, forcing me to deal with the rubble; go fuck yourself.

You know who you are.

Love Letter

I'm grateful for your existence in my life.

No matter if that be past, present, or future.

Whether it's evident or not, you truly have brought out a side of me that I thought was long gone. A side of me that I hid for years and eventually lost because of fear, judgment, there was no space for this version of me, but you allowed me to have that space.

No matter what version of me wanted to shine through that day, you loved me. A piece of me that I wasn't ever sure needed to exist has been brought to light because of you and I think this is one of the many reasons I fell in love.

When we first met, I felt so stuck on you. Patiently waiting for you to spark a conversation because I didn't want to seem too eager. I didn't want to dive into you without knowing how deep the water would be. I was never sure what was drawing me to you so intensely, but you felt comfortable and familiar.

I wanted to be the same for you. I wanted to give you the space to be free and release each version of yourself. Whether that version comes with dark and rainy clouds or burning rays of sunshine. I wanted to be there for it all.

I still do. You are loved, *always*.

Morse Code

You kiss the back of my neck 3 times before you leave.

I convince myself it's morse code for 'i love you'.

Three little words that I can't deliver from my mouth, so I choose not to speak at all.

I've read far too many romance novels to know that this will be trouble. I refuse to spend this life wasting away with mediocre relationships and love stories that end in what ifs.

So, I jump, with no intention of coming up for air.

I want to over analyze this, and you.

I want to indulge in these feelings because love is misunderstood in this generation.

It has little to do with reciprocation.

It's about the memories, the joy, the way you feel more alive than you ever have.

And sure, it can end, and it can feel as if your body is decaying from the inside out, but that's part of the story.

You find love and you let it kill you because then you get to be reborn again.

If this ends in heartache, let it be mine.

No Exit Wound

The worst kind of goodbyes are the ones that enter like a bullet wound and echo through your body months later.

The worst kind of goodbyes are the ones that leave you scratching your skin until the sight of your own blood reminds you that you're alive.

Limits of the Human Body

Research has discovered that the human body can survive for 7 days without water, 45 days without food, and 11 minutes without oxygen.

It's been 48 days without you.

48 days without your physical body next to mine but your scent is stained into my sheets and your little black hairs are tucked in between the floorboards, the same place that you would hide our love when things got too real.

We tore into each other looking for ways to heal our wounds, our darkest moments aligned so perfectly we called it fate.

I'm not willing to retell my story, to open the wounds we sealed in love. I don't want to dance around the dark spots in my mind in hopes that someone new will still love me when they see it.

I don't want to look in the floorboards for anyone else.

Loving you is the last resource on earth,

I can't survive without it.

I Painted Us as Invincible, You Painted Her as Someone Prettier Than Me

I used to get angry at you for not looking at me as if I had put the moon in the sky, but the truth is that being angry at you was easier than loving you more than you will ever love me.

The truth is that I'm angry at myself for not being the type of girl who can be loved like that. For being the type of girl who is incredibly hard to love because of how insecure I am.

I can understand now that it's not easy to love someone who wakes up and avoids mirrors unless it's to alter their appearance to the point of being unrecognizable.

No one wants to fall in love with someone who thinks they are made up entirely of all the parts they hate about themselves.

I am not blind to the fact it's not fair to love someone who will constantly remind you of all the reasons you shouldn't. It's not fair to be hurt over it either.

See, I know now that I can't be angry at you.

I would be a hypocrite.

A Poem About a Boy Who No Longer Thinks About Me

I wish I could have told you not to fall in love with me, not yet.

I wish I shoved the words back down your throat and told you the truth.

I wasn't ready for us.

But I was weak.

So, I did the only thing I knew how to, and I tell you that I love you too.

I let myself fall so hard for you, my heart collapses on itself.

Sometimes it's hard to believe that we've become people who are worlds away from each other now.

Unrequited Love Feels Like Ripping Apart Your Lungs While Trying to Breathe

I expect too much because that's all I know how to give.

I don't understand how others don't have the inherent need to stitch themselves closer to people, to carry around their love like spare change, to go through life without deep conversations and be fine with that.

It's a simple life,

Sure,

But it's not a life that I can shrink myself to be a part of.

How Could A Disaster Like Me Ever Be Worthy of A Boy Like You?

I love you in the way that the night sky holds onto her stars.

It results in her burning herself every single night, but she does it for love.

You love me in the way a lighthouse guides sailors' home; from a distance to avoid getting caught in the waves.

I tell myself that if I tried a little harder, maybe you would understand that my heart beats for you.

We end because you never show up when I ask you to.

It was never about me trying harder, it was about you walking on eggshells around your feelings because then maybe you could avoid catching them.

I could never convince you to love me, or to stay.

But these aren't things you're supposed to convince someone anyways.

One of The Worst Parts About Me Is My Desire to Find Good in Everyone Who Doesn't Deserve It

I know that I write as if you bleed stardust and the sun shines through your eyes because this is the version of you that I want to immortalize.

It's just that I want to paint your soul in neon skylines and tell anyone who is willing to listen about all the ways you have loved me.

I want to believe that when you swallow gasoline and ignite a fire between us with your words, that you don't mean to leave me scarred.

I don't think you're a bad person,

Or I don't think you want to be at least.

It's just that your mother never knew how to hold you and your father forgot how to be one so sometimes you forget to unfold your fists when you try to pull me closer.

Did You Ever Really Love Me or Was I Born into a Body More Sensitive Than the Average Human?

He never wrote songs about me.

We sat up at night for hours, talking about everything in this world except for me.

I spent hours, days, trying to make you feel special.

I wrote novels about you, not caring if the world got tired of hearing about you.

Once, I asked you why you've never written a song about me and all you said was that you didn't know. As if you had spent hours trying to figure out how to put me onto paper.

I tell myself for far too long that no amount of words strung together could possibly explain me.

Truth is, I will never be worth as much as others are to me.

I will always be the one to get hurt.

Soon You Will Realize You Are Just as Flawed as The Rest

You used to cover me with blankets so I'd stop shivering from the open window.

I'm still shivering.

Still smoking your weed by myself at 4 a.m., writing poems high, trying to forget how many things left with your presence.

Still listening to "Stay" on repeat, trying to believe you're coming back like you told me, even though you said things were only okay when we were high.

Your lip-stained beer bottles still rot in my closet, smelling like skeletons and a love that barely existed. I can't get myself to throw them away. I don't want to forget you.

Should I Keep Searching for Meaning in This? We're Going In Circles

You told me that I love with my eyes closed—
Recklessly.

It hurts so badly when we're apart, but the pain doesn't leave when we stay.

I wanted something that would blister and bleed, make me feel like I wasn't as depressed and anxious and fucked up as I felt.

I wanted someone else to feel the hum of light switches turning on and off inside my brain,

but you tried so hard to run this wound under cold water, help me as if I wanted to be helped, soften me when I wanted to be stone.

You used 'I love you's' like Band-Aids that would stop my wounds from bleeding.

You will never want this.

You will never want me screaming lies as if I'm going to fucking kill myself over us, saying anything to make you stay, remembering how it felt to watch someone try to hang themselves over how much I loved you.

We all have barriers.

We all do things to make us feel better.

If The Night Could Talk

(why couldn't you let me fix this?)

You told me we ruined our lives because we met too tender, too inexperienced, too childish for this.

That this love could have worked if I hadn't settled in my last relationship and you knew how to love yourself first; if I believed in hard work instead of soul mates and stopped pretending you would be by my side no matter what.

The universe doesn't draw lines between people. The world is messy and things break because we're not gentle enough.

Anything can work if two people want it badly enough, but the stars can't make people stay.

So, you're right: we've been through too much. but if I met you in another life, I really think we could have been something.

You Left My Body Filled With Land Mines

Tonight, you spend hours picking him off of your body, counting all the places he marked on your skin like petals.

He loves me.

He loves me not. He loves me not. He loves me not.

We Are Set To Destruct In 3.. 2..

You're in my bedroom and *today,* you love me. I'm marking down the days on my calendar till you don't.

I should be happy.

Instead, I've got our heartbreak planned and our plot picked out in my backyard.

I've always needed to know what I'm looking forward to so I can prepare for it and you've always ran at the first sign of a serious commitment.

Let's face it, this love was never meant to last.

'It's okay, I love you' doesn't slide off my tongue as easily as screaming that I hate you.

What's the point in trying if you were never going to stay?

So, I can feel it in my stomach like it's already happened ten times over and my therapist tells me it's called self-sabotaging, but I like to think of it as being alert.

Because eventually we will get tired of screaming and crying and spitting lies about never wanting this in the first place.

If I can't find a way to make you stay, then I sure as hell can find a way to make you leave.

My Fathers Pressure to Be Perfect Weighs on My Chest and I Am Leaking with My Mothers Trust Issues

There's still wounds inside my chest.

Bruises and scars from being too young, too full of regrets that never seem to shut up and I'm trying to pretend they're not there because everyone's lives are better when I'm not sad.

But the truth is growing up is stretching yourself thin until the small things rip through your skin.

Growing up is shedding the armor you've grown to place around your heart.

Growing up is not as glamorous as *being* grown up.

It's staying in your comfort zone until you are shunned from it and don't know what to do anymore. I don't know how to make it not sting.

I'm trying so hard to always do the right thing and I'm learning that sometimes growing up is a gamble of choosing what's hard over what makes you comfortable, because hopefully one day it will be worth it.

Growing up is losing everything that you have ever known but telling yourself that you are going to be better for it.

Time of Death

Saturday 9:22am

You brought me a coffee to work, but what you didn't know was that seeing you did more for me than a caffeine rush ever could.

Sunday 11:22am

I rambled on about astrology and the difference between the signs. I didn't tell you that I already compared our birth charts and our love story was written in the stars.

Search: Is Double Zero Still A Size?

I've been searching the web for ways to get thin fast because maybe if I take up less space then maybe you'll take me back.

If I don't fill the room with words, you can drown me in your thoughts.

Maybe, if I didn't take up so much physical space then you would think I'm enough.

Maybe, if I didn't let my feelings take up too much space, you could fit me inside you.

I can't stop searching for love in places it doesn't exist because I love you.

Why can't you make space for me?

Our Love Could Have Orchestrated Symphonies If You Didn't Love Me When The Lights Were Off And I Loved Myself At The Beginning

Love isn't supposed to sound like a melody created from our shallow breaths and my bloody knees, but I was cursed with the ability to romanticize just about anything.

The same way that you romanticized the wine that spilled from my wrists whenever you told me I wasn't good enough,

Or the galaxies you painted on my skin when the whiskey filled your veins.

Confessions To The Moon

Last weekend I almost called you while I was drunk but I didn't want to bother you. *Anymore.*

I kissed a boy I met at the club but what I didn't tell my friends was that I swallowed my tears when he wasn't looking.

I fell asleep in my best friend's lap, and she told me that I was crying in my sleep the way I used to when we broke up.

Last night I went for a drive and the air felt like it did the first time you kissed me, and I almost crashed the car thinking about what I would do if I got the chance to kiss you one last time.

I watched your favourite movie 4 times today. I don't even like it.

The boy I sit next to in Colour Theory smells like you.

I wanted to call to see how you were doing and ask about your little brothers. Instead, I made peppermint tea.

You left some things at my house, maybe you should pick them up.

Maybe we can grab a coffee.

Maybe we can fall in love again.

I Fell Asleep While You Fell Out Of Love

My heart is beating quicker than it ever should and I can't think about you without the skin falling off my bones and my lungs filling with the tears that I can't help but swallow.

This is supposed to be a poem about love and the way you make me feel like I'm safely wrapped inside a blanket made from stars, but all I can spill out of my mouth is that I feel like I am burning alive.

No one ever tells you that stars aren't as pretty when they are burning inside your throat and you loved me,

you loved me last night but that was 13 hours ago,

and 13 hours doesn't feel like enough time to fall out of love, but you still did it.

So the story goes like this,

we fell asleep in love,

but only one of us woke up the same.

Fight or Flight? Land or Sea?

I choose flight when it comes to others loving me.

It's not that I don't want it, I do. I want to sail out to the middle of the sea and drown in it.

But I've seen enough wreckage in my life to know that I don't want to be the cause of it anymore.

I was born into a haunted lighthouse and the only way I could survive was to build one inside of me.

So, I painted my insides black, and I put up art that made me feel something, and I put far too many locks on all the doors.

The only people who live here are ghosts, and I want your heart to keep beating.

It's Going To Hurt When You Leave Me

It's 3am and you're taking up half the bed, your body wrapped around my pillows.

You're a deep sleeper but I don't want to risk waking you up, so I stay small and quiet and imagine what you're dreaming about.

I wonder if you know that I am completely fascinated by you.

Your pet peeves, how you chew certain things with your mouth open, all down to your favourite colour.

Forest green, to be specific.

So, this is how it's going to go;

A delicate dance between not enough and too much.

But believe me when I say that you are a chance that I will never regret taking.

You Can't Love Me Back to Life, but You Tried

You quoted Perks of Being a Wallflower to me.

You said that I accepted the love that I thought I deserved which broke my heart because you were right.

I thought I was meant to love, not be loved.

So, I accepted whatever came my way.

Until you told me you loved me.

8-year-old me would be jumping up and down in her bed because the man we wished for, the man of our dreams, has just confessed his love.

But 22-year-old me is painting bricks with cement because that is a fairytale that I don't deserve.

You looked at all the dark and twisty parts of my soul and chose to love me despite them.

I don't deserve this, but I want you.

We fall in love, and I beg the universe to let us fall slowly because this was important to me, and important things take time. Something with this much passion, it was inevitable to burn quickly.

I'm used to loving men who weren't ready, and I never imagined I'd become one.

I'm Still In Love, Right Where You Left Me And I Don't Think I'll Be Leaving Anytime Soon

It's been 6 months now and I've convinced myself that you've learned to live without me, to stop loving me, to stop thinking of me when the sky turns pink in the same way my cheeks do when I blush.

You've moved on.

Hell, maybe you've even found someone who dives into love with you and isn't scared that although this is a swimming pool, there may be sharks in the water.

It's been 6 months.

I spent 6 months learning that love must be built on a strong foundation.

I spent 6 months learning that mistakes aren't worth being ashamed of, that screaming and fighting isn't a healthy way to express insecurities.

I spent 6 months working on myself to be better, to love you better, to accept your love better.

So, if you spent 6 months learning to unlove me, then I will spend the next 6 learning to love myself more, to love myself better.

They Never Tell You Where To Put The Things That Leak From Your Chest

Somewhere, by the train station, my heart slipped out of my chest and into your hands.

You wrapped your arms around me and for the first time in my life I couldn't find a single metaphor or word to describe things, so I held those feelings in my hands, and I breathed it all in.

We spent the day wandering the city like two lost lovers, and I kept my fingers curled tightly around it.

What do I do with it now that you're gone?

Our Love Will Last, At Least In These Pages

Okay, so we didn't work.

And I wanted you to stay, I really did.

I never thought that we'd end up the way we did, and I think our story has too many empty pages to really be over, right?

I know some of our memories leave a bad taste in your mouth but love only tastes good with a little bit of pain, right?

I mean, that's why we used to chase tequila with limes, right?

So, I'll stitch together the missed phone calls and the voicemails filled with 'i love you' and I'll put them in a box under my bed marked 'MEMORIES'.

I want to leave things between us still in love, on good terms.

Your Angels Are Watching Over, Day n Nite

The second hospital in this city, the one with the name you refuse to say, is your least favourite.

It's where you remember how heavy rooms can feel with the weight of uncertainty, the pull between worlds.

IV bags drip to the beat of the heart monitors and blood tests leave arms bruised.

All you can hear is the beat of your own heart and all you know how to do is apologize to the worried eyes around you.

<u>Trigger Warning:</u>

The rest of this book may contain topics that are sensitive, uncomfortable, or triggering to read. There is no shame in ending your reading here.

Your mental health comes first, always.

I love you.

Sensitive topics may include but are not limited to parental neglect, LGBT community, sexual assault, self-harm, eating disorders, and other mental health topics.

Selective Apologies

My mother asked me to stop writing about her. She says she's tired of me lying in my poems about her.

I think what she meant to say is that she's too tired to apologize.

My mother told me that I have always had a selective memory. She says I could never remember to clean my room, but I could remember that time she warned me about *becoming a lesbian.*

I think what she meant to say is that she would love me no matter what.

My mother doesn't bring the past up anymore. She says she is tired of arguing and instead she reminds me of all the times that she would check for monsters under my bed.

She says I forgot to write that poem.

I Drink Until I Feel Numb and I Wait Until I Can Feel Numb Again

I still feel every touch my body has endured from demons both years ago and days ago.

Each gentle caress brands my skin as thoughts of safety leave.

My skin is no longer pure, this body is no longer my ~~home~~ own.

REMINDER: Your Childhood Sits Inside of You Like Russian Nesting Dolls, Be Kind to Them

Each time I skip meals because my body feels too big to justify anything else, I remember her.

When I trace the parts of my body with a razor, fantasizing about where to cut off the extras, *I remember her.*

When my face starts to change, my hips start to widen, *I remember her.*

The little girl who didn't have an answer when the teachers asked, "what do you want to be when you grow up?" because she knew she couldn't tell them that she didn't want to grow up or that this body has never felt at home to her.

I remember the little girl who is 6, but also 7, and 8, and 9, who sits inside of me like Russian nesting dolls, aching to be something more or nothing at all.

The little girl who tore herself apart with her mother's razor blades searching to feel anything else.

I try to be the person that little girl needed when she was 6 and didn't understand why it mattered who she grew up to love,

when she was 8 and happy until her doctor told her that she was taking up too much space,

and when she was 15 and alone so 'one-night stands' were interchangeable with 'somewhere warm to sleep for the night.'

That little girl deserved better.

That little girl is still inside and I want to make her proud.

This Body Has Been Contaminated With Roaming Hands

It's coming up soon.

The day it happened.

The day that he stole a piece of me.

A piece of my mind, *my peace of mind.*

A part of me that I didn't understand could be taken away.

Everyone tells me that it isn't my fault, then whose fault is it?

They tell me that it's going to go away.

"You'll get justice".

They never tell me what I can do until that day comes.

How do I deal with that pain? Where do I put this?

~~Victim~~ Impact Statement

They asked me to write a letter of impact.

They don't understand that arranging and rearranging the letters of the alphabet can never properly articulate what was taken from me.

I've been guarded and fearful in ways I never imagined, words I would never have associated myself with days ago.

My doctor prescribed me a cocktail of medications but there isn't any concoction of pills that can erase the triggers.

It doesn't make the panic attacks stop. It doesn't make me feel comfortable around men.

It doesn't take anything back.

I don't know how to tell my friends that hugs feel like tornados wrapping around my body, that any form of physical touch is no longer my love language.

His roaming hands have forced me to look for the glowing red exit signs in every room I enter.

I have a distant memory of showers being 10 minutes long. I spent hours scrubbing him off my skin, telling myself that if the water isn't leaving blisters that I must not be clean enough yet.

If The Night Could Talk

I still feel the burning of the unwanted handprints
pushing down on my skin and into my bones, the swabs
for DNA that did not belong to my body, the cameras
flashing in my eyes, the cold touch of the examination
tools because this body is now a crime scene.

These sensations can't be washed away with lavender
soap and rags.

These memories can't be erased with anti-depressants.

I read once that it takes 7 years for your entire body to
regenerate new cells.

If that's true, then in 1,025 days my body will have
never experienced his hands. I remind myself of this.

In 1,026 days, I will be okay. An extra for good measure.

I remind myself that I can never be the girl I was before,
but I will be a better woman.

I will find my voice again.

Locked Doors Feel Safer Than You Ever Did

My parents taught me that emotions were something to be afraid of.

Something to bury until you were alone behind closed doors, and no one could bare witness to them. I learned to shut myself in my room whenever I felt myself slipping under the weight of emotions that I didn't understand.

I was ashamed of my emotions by grade 5.

When I was 16, I couldn't leave my bedroom door open anymore because it felt too vulnerable. The sound of my door closing, the lock settling into place, it was the sound of safety.

I'm 22 now and I know it's okay to feel sad, I'm allowed to slip when no one is watching and can cut themselves on my shattered pieces.

But I am not allowed to open that door or tell you how I feel unless it is from a logical standpoint.

I know I can't change the past, I can't break this habit, but I can't help but wonder what would happen if one day my parents knocked on my door to ask me how I feel.

A Letter I Never Wanted To Write

I remember when I was a little girl, I thought my Dad was the funniest person to exist.

Every weekend I would be excited to laugh at his jokes and silly faces.

But I don't recall a single memory of a time that we shared a meaningful moment.

I remember the conversations of my mother's addiction, and the disappointments that followed.

I remember being painted in expectations that I didn't understand yet.

But mostly, I remember all the times that he had to go to work and come back just to be too tired to spend time with me.

I remember asking him to teach me how to play guitar, I just wanted to spend time with him, but he was too busy.

Dad, I remember having you around, but I never really remember you being there.

And now, Dad, I understand why I hide behind humor. I understand why I close the best parts of myself off from boys.

If The Night Could Talk

It's easier if you don't get too close to them.

I've wanted nothing more than to be close to you,

but I never felt like you needed that because you
already had a daughter who made you proud.

A daughter who didn't come from a failed relationship.

And that's the only form of love that I'm familiar with.

The kind that doesn't really feel like love at all.